VICKI LANSKY

WELCOMING YOUR SECOND BABY

Revised and Updated
3rd edition

illustrations by Jane Prince

BOOK PEDDLERS
MINNETONKA, MN

DISTRIBUTED TO THE BOOK TRADE BY
PUBLISHERS GROUP WEST

Special editorial thanks to:
Kathryn Ring, Toni Burbank, Sandra L. Whelan, Julie Surma, Francie Paper and Abby Rabinovitz.

The contents of this book have been reviewed for accuracy and appropriateness by Jan Goodwalt, R.N., of the St. Paul Hospital, and Joan Reivich of Philadelphia's Booth Maternity Center. Material for children at a birth has been reviewed and enhanced by Penny Simkin and Jeanine Bontrager. Thanks also to Dr. Burton White for his comments.

Special thanks to the parents who shared their words and feelings. Their quotes are reprinted with permission from *Vicki Lansky's* Practical Parenting™ newsletter published from 1979 to 1987.

We appreciate the right to reprint: "Some Things Don't Make Any Sense at All," by Judith Viorst. Reprinted with the permission of Atheneum Publishers from *If I Were in Charge of the World and Other Worries* © 1981 by Judith Viorst.

WELCOMING YOUR SECOND BABY

A BANTAM BOOK (August 1984)
Book Peddlers *Revised 3rd Edition* June 2005

NEW 13 ISBN: 978-1-931863-44-5

ISBN 0-931863-44-X

For reprint permission, group sales or quantity discounts contact:
BOOK PEDDLERS
2828 Hedberg Drive • Minnetonka, MN 55305
(952) 544-1154 • fax (952) 544-1153
www.bookpeddlers.com & www.practicalparenting.com

09 10 11 12   7 6 5 4

printed in China

Contents

Introduction: *A Welcome Addition*

A New Addition

❧

If you are a sibling, you know how your sister or brother can be annoying and difficult, or adoring and dependable. If you don't have one, you probably wish you did.

Having a second child is exciting but sometimes seems a bit overwhelming to parents. The first has already taken so much of your love, time, and attention, so much of the space in your home, so much of your income, that you wonder how you'll possibly manage. And you wonder, perhaps, if you'll ever be able to love a second child as much as you do the first. Will there be enough love for both? Are you being disloyal to your firstborn by forcing a sibling on him or her? Will your second child be an intruder in your family, a competitor for your attention and love? In short, will your second child be a welcome addition?

You know that a new child will bring your firstborn down to earth a bit, teach about sharing, and provide a live-in playmate in childhood.

Two things you can plan on for sure are that your second child will not be a replica of the first, even though they may look alike, and that you can't predict, totally, the reception of the second by the first. Whatever the age of the first, whatever the spacing between the two, the firstborn may adore or be unhappy about the baby; may grow up in amazing ways or regress to babyhood; may be fascinated by or indifferent to the baby. Of course some part of the older child's reception of the baby will depend upon his or her age, on how dependent your child has been on you, and on his or her emotional maturity, but some aspects of the reception and acceptance are simply unexplainable, a matter of personality and the circumstances of the moment.

I've included many ideas to help you help your child adjust to the arrival of the new baby. You'll find lots of good ones here but please, don't feel you need to try them all! There is such a thing as too much of a good thing. You can over-prepare your child by too much attention to preparation.

By the way, don't forget to have yourself prepared—for childbirth, that is. Take that refresher course you don't think you have time for. It will really help. Trust me, you really don't remember it all. Plus, it's good quality time for you and your partner.

Children without siblings have been rated as having poorer social skills. Children with sibs are said to be better at forming and maintaining friendships; getting along with people who are different; expressing feelings in a positive way and showing sensitivity to the feelings of others. To achieve this, you, the parent, will now have to live through years of sibling conflicts and jealously, which will never bother your children as much as it will bother you. Whether or not this rating system is accurate, only you can say.

But I think the best part of having one's second child is letting you see more clearly how each child comes with their set of 'stuff' (*personality and the like*) for which you can not claim responsibility or credit. And as these small people emerge into big people, you will share a journey that is really second to done.

Relax. Enjoy your first child. Enjoy your pregnancy. The best is yet to come!

Vicki Lansky

SOME THINGS DON'T MAKE ANY SENSE AT ALL

by Judith Viorst

My mom says I'm her sugarplum,
My mom says I'm her lamb.

My mom says I'm completely perfect
Just the way I am.

My mom says I'm a super-special
wonderful terrific little guy.

My mom just had another baby.

Why?

CHAPTER ONE

How Can I Best Prepare Our Child for the Birth of a New Baby?

Your first step, obviously, is to announce that the baby's on the way. The "whens" and "hows" of this depend not only on the age of your first child, but also on that child's interest in the event and relative maturity. Each child will handle the news differently, in his or her own unique way, no matter how you prepare your child. And the child who is initially pleased about becoming a big sister or brother may have a change of heart once the baby is born, or even six months after that.

No matter what your child's age, don't be surprised, if after you share the big news, your child just drops the subject for a while.

Exactly when you tell your child will depend to a large extent on the child's age. A pregnancy that seems long enough to you will be a lifetime to a child whose concept of time is still fuzzy.

We worry not only about our child's acceptance of the new baby, but also about our own. *(Will I ever be able to love this child as much as my first one?)* We fall in love with each child in a different way and at a different pace. Don't worry. It does happen in the natural sequence of things.

When to Share Your Great News With Your Child

• Ideally, tell a preschooler about two or three months before the birth, but realistically, you'll be sharing the news once you've made it public. You may be pushed into telling an observant child who notices that Mom is getting "fat."

• Don't tell any child until you're ready for the whole world to know. A child can't be expected to keep such a secret.

• Be careful of telling a child too soon, in the event of a miscarriage. The child might feel responsible in some way for the loss of the baby. If you decide to tell the child right away, be sure to offer full and honest explanations if problems arise later.

• Don't wait too long to tell any child. He or she may overhear you talking about your pregnancy, or a friend or neighbor may let the word slip. Your child could become unduly worried because you're always tired or occasionally sick without explanation. The boredom of waiting a long time for the baby to come is not as bad for the child as is the feeling that something strange and secret is going on.

• When explaining to a young child about when the baby is due, tie the birth to an event instead of to a month or week—"after Christmas," or "during your spring vacation from nursery school"—but don't pinpoint it too exactly.

Preparing Your Child for Life With a New Baby

• Don't tell a child of any age how he or she is going to feel about the baby. Statements like "You're going to love the baby," and "You're going to have lots of fun playing with the baby and helping me care for the baby" may express your heart's desires, but might only serve to irritate your child or set him or her up for conflict if your child doesn't feel the way you predicted.

• Stress the positive and give your child a feeling of status by saying things like, "You're going to be a big brother," rather than, "You're going to have a baby brother or sister."

• Take advantage of the unknown sex of the baby to encourage nonsexist thinking by pointing out that "Girls can _____ too," and "Boys can _____ too." (You may see a bit of jealousy already developing if your child wants the baby to be of the opposite sex from himself or herself.)

• Stress the fact, especially to a young child, that the gender of the unborn baby will be a surprise. (If you have had an ultrasound, sonogram or an amniocentesis and already know the baby's sex, that's a different matter!)

• Let your child fantasize about the baby by drawing pictures of how he or she thinks it will look. The drawings may offer you an opportunity to correct misconceptions or provide explanations.

• "Borrow" a baby, or babysit one regularly, with two thoughts in mind. First, your child will see how infants act and how much care they need, and second, you'll have a chance to practice having more than one to care for. (And perhaps the other mother will owe you some babysitting time when your second baby is born!)

• Better yet, expose your child to more than one infant. Young ones, especially, sometimes have trouble imagining a sibling similar, but not identical, to a baby they've seen.

• Let your child see a nursing mother, if possible, so that if you breast-feed, it won't seem strange.

• Don't let the child think the newborn will be a playmate; be clear about the fact that they do little but eat, sleep, and cry.

• Talk about the different things your older child will show or teach the new baby once it is "out."

• Share child care with your spouse (if you don't already) so your child won't expect mother's care exclusively.

• Point out pictures of newborns in magazines to prepare your child for the way an infant looks. Explain that babies have no teeth, and that there will be a scab where the umbilical cord was.

• Also point out older babies, to let your child know that newborn babies do change as they grow.

Know that giving rational explanations of an impending future event to a child under the age of 2 will not be understood.

Creative Art Projects for You and Your Child to Make to Welcome the New Baby

- A WELCOME SIGN to put up the day the baby comes home. When you know the name, use it—or add it—on the sign.

- ANNOUNCEMENT art: a sign for the house, a note for neighbors and friends, etc.

- QUIET, BABY SLEEPING signage to put on a door or hang from a door knob.

- WALL ART to decorate baby's room.

- ART WORK to wrap gifts for the baby.

- T-SHIRT MESSAGE. Using a plain white t-shirt, let a child decorate it or color on it after you first write with fabric paint any of the following:
  1) I'm *(baby x's)* Big Sister/Brother
  2) I am the Big Sister/Brother
  3) I'm Going to be a Big Sister/Brother Soon
     (*an announcement t-shirt*)

Promoting Self-esteem for the New Big Brother or Sister

• Check with your hospital, doctor, or childbirth instructor to see if sibling classes are offered in your area for children whose parents are expecting. Such classes, appropriately geared to children's ages, can be very helpful.

• Let your child come with you to checkups and have those questions your child may have, answered. Ultrasound images can be shared with the soon-to-be sibling.

• Don't deprive your toddler of your attention, but don't go overboard in the other direction, either. Go out with your spouse reasonably often (with a reliable sitter in charge, of course) and insist on some quiet time for yourself, all to help prepare your child for the future new demands there will be on your time.

• If you don't send your child to preschool, daycare or a play group, this might be the time to start. At the very least your child will be comfortable in an out-of-the-house setting. You may want to start your own as a way of preparing your child to being around other kids.

• Don't pile on too many gifts and treats before the birth (or after it either), or you'll be sending a guilt-laden message to your child.

• Get out your photos or movies and spend time together looking at pictures of your child as an infant.

• Make big changes, such as moving the child to a big bed, completing toilet training, or giving up the bottle, well before the baby's expected birth, so the child will feel that he or she is growing up, not being pushed aside (see regression, page 73).

TIPS FOR MOVING UP TO A BIG BED

As a rule of thumb, a child thirty-six inches tall is big enough for a big bed.

• Let your child start with a pillow while still in the crib. It helps children learn how to center themselves while asleep.

• Set up the full size bed while the crib is still up, and let your child first nap there and then read stories together there. Let your child choose where to sleep for a few weeks.

• Does the room allow for a full or queen-size bed? Less chance of rolling off...more room for snuggles and family time. Using a trundle bed? Let the child sleep in the lower 'trundle' section at first.

• Limit roll-off problems by: putting the mattress (or even the crib mattress) on the floor; pushing the bed up against a wall and placing cushions on the floor on the open side; or use a removable side-rail for a few weeks.

• Let your child pick out sheets for the new 'grown-up' bed.

• Celebrate the switch with a 'big bed' party. Family members can bring new stuffed animals for the event.

Other Ways to Help Prepare Your Child for the Baby's Birth

• Speak of the baby as *our* family's, not as *yours* or *mine*.

• Get a baby doll for your toddler if he or she doesn't have one, or outfit an old one with new clothes and some new equipment. Be sure the doll is immersible; it will probably undergo some bathing later!

• Unpack your child's old baby clothes together and recall stories about infancy while you do.

• Take your child with you to shop for a new baby outfit.

• Consider, if you take down the crib, not just moving it to another room but storing it away for a while. A child's bed is very personal. You might even want to paint it a different color so it won't stir up memories (and resentments). If you are just moving it to another room, do so well in advance of your due date. Or trade crib or stroller items with a friend so it doesn't seem like the new baby is "taking" things.

• Let your preschooler in on your discussion of the baby's name as well as other plans and decisions. Listen and talk about them but don't make promises about selecting his or her choice of the baby's name. You might consider using it as a nickname.

• Have your child talk to the baby using your navel as a microphone.

• Let your child feel the baby kicking and listen to the heartbeat with a stethoscope. Some toy stethoscopes work surprisingly well.

> *Our 2-1/2-year-old always knew we were getting ready to leave him when we gathered up the pillows for our childbirth classes. He'd immediately throw a full-scale tantrum, going so far as to hold his breath and pass out. We'd go anyway, knowing from hard experience that he'd come to and be all right with the sitter. But I must admit that leaving the house with our child purple and unconscious on the floor pretty much took the fun out of it.*
>
> *Ellen S., Minneapolis, MN*
>
> *My 5-year-old daughter would talk to the baby putting her mouth close to my belly button. (Since the baby was inside me I could hear what replies he was thinking and tell her.) The baby would get furious if someone was mean to her, and the baby would take her side.*
>
> *C. Calzada, Miami, FL*

• Invite your child to do stretching and muscle-strengthening exercises with you. Leg raises and pelvic rocks are usually especially appealing for little people.

• Take your child with you to prenatal checkups. With subsequent visits to the doctor, your child will likely come up with additional questions. Children will often mull over earlier questions and answers; doctor's visits offer a place to ask for more information.

Does Spacing Affect Adjustment?

We feel the most important help our older child had was a good three years of our attention before she had a sibling. This got her off to a good start and almost eliminated any rivalry problems we might have had.

Candace Waidrum, Paris, TX

Our son Matt was 19 months old when we brought his new brother, Patrick, home. His first hello was to jump into the baby's crib while it was occupied. Things got steadily worse until big brother made the adjustment of sharing Mom and Dad. Somehow Patrick has managed to survive a year and eight months, and a change has gradually taken place. The little kid who used to just lie there is suddenly lots of fun.

Mac Ann Koenigsfeld, Charles City, IA

Our children are four and one-half years apart. Our oldest had a "full turn" at being a baby and fully welcomed his sister. Now, at 10-1/2 and 6, they seem to be secure in their own persons.

Betsy Durham, Waterford, CT

My brother and I were 18 months apart and great buddies, but I still remember the desire for more individual attention. My children are eight years apart, and both have benefited from individual attention—but are not buddies at all. I doubt there is an ideal spacing.

Beverly Audeh, Huntsville, AL

Preparing a 1-Year-Old Child for a New Baby

Sorry to mislead you but there really is nothing you can do to prepare a young "older" sibling for the baby's arrival. Yes, let your child participate in new baby preparations, but don't assume it will be meaningful.

Having two children under two years of age will press you with physical as well as emotional demands. Keep in mind that this has been handled by many before you and that you too will come through with flying colors. While it will be more tiring in the beginning, your children—closer in age—will be better playmates for each other and you'll be done with diapers and baby stuff sooner rather than later.

Rather than trying to make your first child grow up faster, it will probably do better for everyone if you just lower your expectations and let your toddler be "babyish" too. Rather than trying to prepare your child for the baby or explain the birthing process, try to spend extra time enjoying your older child.

Preparing Your Older Child or Teenager

• Look upon your pregnancy as an excellent opportunity to read about and discuss human sexuality, reproduction, and family life with your child. Sign up online for weekly in utero developmental information by e-mail at places such as www.babyzone.com.

• Don't insist that your youngster read straight through every book you supply. Leave books and magazine articles in convenient places for casual (and private) scanning.

• To help your children understand how difficult it is for you to pick up things left on the floor, strap a large stuffed animal or pillow around their waist, and then ask them to help you pick up toys.

• Don't make your older child dread the baby's birth by talking a great deal about how much help he or she is going to be.

• Give a special "baby notebook" to a child who would enjoy keeping a journal and designate him or her as the "Baby Reporter."

• Let your child help you compile a list of people and their phone numbers who he or she can be responsible for calling to announce when the new baby is born.

• Prepare yourself to deal with the fact that your teenager may be embarrassed about the fact that you are pregnant and that there will be an infant in the family. Talk about any other families you know who have "late" babies and point out the fun they have.

When the New Baby Arrives

• Make every effort to hire or enlist household and/or new baby help so you can spend some one-on-one time with your older "baby" daily, or at least weekly. It's a good investment in your family life.

• Make time for yourself, even if it's only a half hour of privacy or a nap. If you fall apart, you're no good to either child.

Preparing Your Pet for a New Baby

Whether your pet is a long time family resident or new since the birth of your first child, you'll find your pet will have to make accommodations for a new baby in the house. A pet, like a child, may be put out more often by the changes in their routine than actual jealousy of the baby.

• Before bringing your baby home, take your pet to the vet for a routine health exam and necessary vaccinations. If you've been planning on neutering or de clawing your pet, do so before the baby arrives. Have your pets get use to having their nails clipped on a regular basis.

• Be sure your dog is free of fleas. A trip to the groomer in your last month or while you're at the hospital might be helpful.

• Allow your pet to explore and investigate baby items and furnishings before the baby arrives. You might even send home a receiving blanket or a piece of the baby's clothing from the hospital before the baby comes home to introduce your baby's scent to your pet.

• Invite friends with babies and toddlers to visit during your pregnancy so your pet can spend some time around "little people."

• Don't let a cat get use to sleeping in the baby's crib. Discourage a pet from jumping into the baby's bed or changing table by applying double-stick tape to some of the surfaces.

• Dogs, more than cats, can be disturbed by a baby's cries. Make a recording of a crying baby during your pregnancy—(you probably have at least one friend with a crying baby who can accommodate you!)—and play it occasionally. Stroke your dog and speak in soothing sounds while the tape is played.

• If a baby's room is off-limits to your pooch, you may wish to invest in a baby gate. If this is true for your cat, you may wish to install a screen door.

• Reward a dog for good behavior when around your newborn.

Sharing Age-Appropriate Reproductive Information

• Show your readiness to answer questions about birth and reproduction by your tone of voice and your patience. Give assurance that it's all right to ask any question.

• Use the correct words for the parts and functions of the body in your discussions. They're no harder to learn than other words, and they won't have to be unlearned later. (For instance, use the word *uterus*, not stomach.)

• Get suitable books about babies and birth very early in your pregnancy, perhaps even before you break the news to your child. Read them together and make them available for casual perusal by the child (see page 16).

• Don't be surprised if your child aged 2 or so has no questions, or very few, about the baby. A statement like, "Mothers have a special place where the baby grows until it's ready to be born" may be all that's required in the way of explaining reproduction.

• Be prepared to repeat whatever facts you do give many times.

• Expect lots of questions from your preschooler. He or she will probably want details about "what's going on inside there"—how the baby eats, sleeps, goes to the bathroom, and other such practical information. Try not to answer more than what's asked.

• On the other hand, don't be alarmed if your preschooler doesn't ask any questions. For some children, the baby doesn't seem real until it actually appears. Often children need the physical presence of the baby before they become interested and start asking questions.

> *We showed our child pictures of intrauterine development, and took him to childbirth films. He saw a sex education special on PBS. If we had it to do over, we would not prepare him so well. We put too much emphasis on the new baby, and he reacted.*
>
> *Dana Clark, Santa Barbara, CA*
>
> *When our last child was on the way, our girls were 7 and 8. I bought two very good books with lots of pictures explaining the hows and whys of birth. They loved seeing how "their" baby was developing. They were as excited as my husband and I were. It's been three years now, and the poor "baby" has had three mothers—he can't get away with much!*
>
> *Susan Lipke, Harietta, MI*

• If you have the feeling that your child is taking an "if-I-ignore-it-it-will-go-away" attitude, you may want to introduce the subject yourself, so he or she will realize that the baby is real and really will be arriving.

• For a child who is old enough to ask or understand, explain the stretching of a mother's vagina by putting a tennis ball into a tube sock to show how the sock's opening easily stretches and then resumes its original opening.

"The Birds & the Bees" Books

Your pregnancy is the perfect time to share re-productive information with your child and read-together books are the easiest place to start. As with any book, the most important message is the one conveyed by your reading of it. No book has to be read in its entirety. Children will express interest in different information at different ages. Take time to ask and answer questions that arise as you read. At first you may be uncomfortable answering some questions correctly, but it's worth doing.

Cute terminology or relying on the concepts from animal and plant life may do everyone more of a disservice than not. As adults, we don't always use the correct physical terms ourselves, but the more we use these words, the more comfortable we become with them and the more comfortable our children become, too. Don't let old outdated embarrassments get in the way.

The most impressive book on in-utero development is ***A Child Is Born*** by Lennart Nilsson. In the latest edition of this classic (originally published almost 40 years ago), photographer Nilsson shares a remarkable group of in-utero pictures. It is fascinating reference to the process of human development.

There is also an edition of this book using these photographs but with text written by Sheila Kitzinger that many feel is more appropriate to share with children 6 and up. It is called ***Being Born***. Regardless of which edition you use, the images are fascinating to parents and child.

Now you can view many of these same photographs online by just going to: www.americanbaby.com/home/fetal-development.html. (Click on *'pictures of the fetus.'*)

There are books for just about every sensibility and age. Many parents buy more than one to offer more than one perspective. Here are other books worth looking for:

How Your Were Born by Joanna Cole & Margaret Miller
A simple text explains prenatal development from conception to birth. The pictures explain cell division and growth in-utero at 3, 6 and 9 months as well as the birth process. Color photographs of different families illustrate new baby behavior and family joy. For ages 3-6.

"Where Did I Come From?" by Peter Mayle
This large-format book calls itself "the facts of life without any nonsense." Its ap-

proach is humorous and frank, its colored illustrations cartoon-like. The aim is to
have fun with the subject, and it covers lovemaking, orgasm, conception, and growth
inside the womb using the same humorous approach. For ages 6-9.

Before You Were Born: *A Lift-the-Flap Book* by Jennifer Davis.
This book has whimsical yet accurate drawings in this book of prenatal development told in rhyme. It is a story told from a pregnant mom's point of view. For
ages 4-8.

Mommy Laid an Egg! or Where Do Babies Come From? by Babette Cole.
This is a direct but light hearted book that communicates the essentials but
with humor. The parents make up absurd tales and they are corrected by their
children. For ages 4-8.

***First Comes Love: All About the Birds and the Bees and Alligators, Possums &
People, To***o by Jennifer Davis and Claire Mackie/illustrator.
This spirited book in rhyme and color drawings introduces the facts of life and how
we all got here. For ages 4-8.

Why Boys and Girls are Different by Carol Greene.
This is a simple introduction to sex for preschoolers from a Christian point of view.
For ages 3-5.

Baby Face(s)

Small children *LOVE* pictures of babies. What better way to introduce the subject. There are many wonderful books that show pictures of babies which your child can enjoy now and your new baby will enjoy later. Take advantage of this natural interest when introducing the idea of a new baby in your household.

Your bookstore, library or online bookstore has many. Check them out. Here are just a few titles to get you started:

Oh Baby by Sara Stein. This 36 page book of color photos of new babies shares close ups as they grow and develop during year one.

Baby Faces (LOOK BABY! BOOKS) by Margaret Miller.

Smile (BABY FACE BOARD BOOK, NO 2) by Roberta Grobel Intrater.

Or make your own "book" by using pictures of your own baby, or faces of babies in your family or neighborhood. Or even of those cut from a magazine. It's easy to fill a 4x6-inch plastic photo album and then the pictures are easy to enjoy and safe in your baby's hands. The more faces, the better.

CHAPTER TWO

How Can I Help Our Child Adjust to My Absence While I'm in the Hospital?

The younger your child is, and the less often he or she has been left with others in your absence, the longer any hospital stay will seem to the child whose time perception isn't well developed. Today with the little time new parents spend in the hospital often it seems there is hardly time to miss mom, especially if the new baby arrived in the middle of the night and familiar people spent the next day at the older child's home. Yet you never know if your stay may end up being a longer one. One 8-year-old, when asked how long his mother was in the hospital to have her baby, responded "a month." In fact, she was there only four days.

Some parents try to go out a little more often during the pregnancy and some take a short "for-parents-only" trip or two as a sort of rehearsal. The main preparation is to make sure your child knows exactly what will happen while mom's in the hospital—where he or she will be eating and sleeping and who will be in charge and that mom's hospital stay won't be very long.

When asked who will care for them when mom goes to the hospital, most children will say "dad." Since dad will no doubt be in the delivery room with mom, children need to understand it will probably NOT be dad.

Taking your child to a hospital-sponsored sibling-to-be class is a good way to introduce the hospital concept and the people who work there. It may also help convince him or her that the hospital is a good place with good people, not a place to be dreaded or feared. Sibling classes for children ages 3-10 help them understand the mechanics of birth and explore their feelings about a new baby. The class will tour the maternity ward, see a new born and a hospital room where mom will be.

Check with your hospital as early as possible about their policy for having children visit the maternity floor. Most hospitals do allow this now, unless there are special circumstances. If children aren't allowed, you can perhaps plan to visit with your child in the lobby or lounge.

Preparing Your Child for Your Hospital Stay

• Try to take your child with you for one or more of your regular checkups, perhaps to hear the baby's heartbeat, see the ultrasound, and to meet the doctor and nurses, and see the office where you visit so often.

• Take the child to the hospital you'll be going to. Have lunch and visit the gift shop. If you can, visit the maternity floor and let the child peek into a room to see how you'll be living while you're there. Point out a phone in a room or in the hall, and say that's where you'll be calling from when you call home. Discuss what his or her visit to you in the hospital will be like.

• Explain very carefully to your child what will happen while you're in the hospital—where he or she will be staying, and who will do the caretaking. The best plan may be to keep your child at home with a relative, or a familiar babysitter. The more normal things are, the less difficult it will be for your child.

• Explain an alternative plan for the day or night you leave for the hospital, if there's any possibility you'll have to make changes (if a scheduled sitter can't be reached, for example).

• Tell your child about the possibility that Mommy may go to the hospital while he or she is asleep or at school. Discuss who will be there with your child when this occurs.

Before You Go to the Hospital

• Record some favorite bedtime stories for your young child, to be played while you're gone. (And don't forget to say "good night" at the end!)

• Put a picture of yourself in your child's room. And have your child pick out a photo for you to take to the hospital so the new baby can "see" his or her older sibling.

• Ask your child to take care of something for you while you're gone—your favorite scarf, a piece of jewelry or pottery—and decide together where the best place in your child's room is to keep it.

• Tell your child you'll call every day from the hospital. For a child old enough to use the phone, write down the hospital number. Don't assume you can use your cell phone. Many hospitals don't allow their use.

• Make a few practice calls when you're away from home to familiarize your child with your telephone voice if speaking on the phone with you is new for your child.

• Hide a few small gifts around the house. When you call from the hospital, you'll be able to tell your child where to look for them.

• Make or buy a little welcome present (such as a bib) for the sibling to give to the new baby when you come home.

• Give your child plenty of occasions to get used to whoever will care for him or her while you're gone. If the child will be staying with Grandma or another relative or friend, set up an overnight visit so the house and bedroom will be familiar.

> _I was at home during most of my labor and this upset my two boys—perhaps better to go to the hospital sooner. They visited me the next day in the hospital and found it hard to understand why I couldn't come home right away!_
>
> _Mrs. H. Skinner, N. Vancouver, B.C._

Shortly Before the Baby is Due

• Let your child help you pack your hospital bag and think of things to put in.

• Tell your child that, yes, you are going to the hospital, but you are also coming back.

• Select a photo of your child and let him or her know it will be placed in your room in the hospital where you can easily see it.

• Get the child to make you some drawings to help decorate the hospital room.

• Before you go (and for your convenience when you get home), keep up with the laundry; stock your cupboards with staples; and freeze casseroles, breads, and desserts for future use. It's okay to just load up on frozen dinners, too.

• Write thank-you notes for baby gifts as promptly as you can; you won't have so many to do after the baby is born when you're busier than ever.

• Have a "practice day," with mom resting in her room while the rest of the family fends for itself. (More power to you if you can pull this one off!)

• Make a "birthday" cake with your older child and freeze it. When you and the new baby arrive home, defrost the cake and have a small party for the birth of the baby.

When You're in the Hospital

• Make frequent calls to your child. They needn't be lengthy. Talk about the baby, but not exclusively, and don't forget the most important message: "I love you, and I'll be home soon."

• Use an instant or digital camera and send home a photo of the baby, one of you with the baby, and another of you alone. If your cell phone has a camera, you can use it for this too.

• Ask your child to be responsible for watering or helping to water certain plants at home.

When Your Child Visits You at the Hospital

• Don't build up your child's visit to the hospital in case a visit isn't possible for some reason.

• Remember your child is anxious to see you—not the baby.

• Don't allow other guests when your child visits you. Let the first visit, at least, be for family only.

• Greet your child *without* your new infant in your arms.

• Have a gift "from the baby" at the hospital for the older child.

• Let the nurse present a baby doll (which you brought with you) to your child, so he or she can have a "baby" from the hospital too.

• Take a small soft toy to the hospital as a gift for the new baby from the older sibling. Keep it in the baby's nursery crib to help your child recognize the new baby brother or sister in the nursery.

• Take photos of your child and the new baby together.

• Take the photo of your child with the new baby to be developed at a photo shop that transfers photos on to custom t-shirts. You may want to add a line below the photo such as, " Jennifer's Big Brother".

• Ask the nurse to tape a photo of the big sister or brother on the baby's bassinet to make the baby easier to find when looking in the nursery window.

• Plan your child's hospital visit at the time of day when he or she is not hungry or tired.

• Have the person who brought your child to the hospital for the visit take him or her home—especially if it's dad—to avoid another separation.

• Let your child hold the new baby. But don't be surprised if the older child's attention span is brief and there is more interest in the mobility of your hospital bed than in the baby.

• Be prepared for your young child to cry when it's time to leave, or to show anger at you for being away from home. A crying jag or tantrum is understandable in light of what seems to your child a very long separation from you. Don't be embarrassed—the hospital staff is accustomed to this type of behavior.

Coming Home

• Let your child come with dad to pick you up at the hospital, if it works for everyone.

• If the child is home when you arrive from the hospital, try to have someone else carry the baby into the house. Pay special attention to your older child for at least a few minutes.

• Put a 24-hour moratorium on visitors. The first day home is another day for family only.

• Plan to spend your first day home with everyone in bed for the day.

• Or arrange for the child to visit someone and be brought home after you and the baby are settled. If you do this, devote your full attention to the child for as long as possible when he or she comes home.

• Be prepared for your child to express conflicting emotions in response to the baby. He or she may be surprised (despite your warnings) that the baby cries so much and doesn't seem to understand anything.

• Plan to indulge yourself, if at all possible, with cleaning help, an occasional baby-sitter to play with your older child, or a whole day in bed when dad's home. Don't fall into the trap of believing that you're indispensable and that nothing will be done right unless you do it. Relax and accept help gratefully when it's offered.

• If dad can take paternity leave, it should start now! There is lots more to do with two children.

Some children have been known to be happy, angry, sad or to even disregard mom's and/or baby's arrival home from the hospital. Don't be hurt if you experience a reception of little interest or downright indifference. It's often a mask for feelings of abandonment.

> *My son, then 2-1/2, didn't really understand what was about to happen even though it was carefully explained. On the way out of the hospital he was in my lap in the wheelchair and the new baby was held by the nurse, not by Mommy or Daddy.*
>
> *Jerri Oyama, Northbridge, CA*
>
> *My husband captured the moment of their meeting, and we now have a document of our 3-year-old's response to meeting his younger brother. It's priceless.*
>
> *Diane Phillips, Milwaukee, WI*

Gender Baby Blues

Whether you find out from your ultrasound or wait until delivery, most parents usually have hopes as to the sex of one's unborn child. It is a natural part of pregnancy. Parents who already have one child or more of one sex understandably experience feelings that are stronger in expectation of a specific sex than first time parents. Yet parents are often unprepared for having a child of the opposite sex from what they had hoped for. It's normal to feel disappointment, failure, resentment and then feelings of guilt for all of these feelings. If this is your reaction, realize that you're not alone. But it is important to resolve these feelings as quickly as possible. Consider getting help with overcoming them so as not to affect your relationship with your new baby.

Children, too, often have gender preferences. A child asking for a same sex sibling is in all likelihood just asking for a playmate. A child asking for an opposite sex sibling may fear competition, believing an opposite sex sibling will pose less of a threat. But even then, that might not be the case. Sometimes a preference is verbalized by a child from something as minor as a statement overheard from another child.

Reassure your child that no matter what the sex of the new baby is, he or she won't be replaced by this new family member. Also verbalize that boys and girls are able to do the same things.

CHAPTER THREE

What If We Want Our Child to Be Present at the Birth of the Baby?

Parents who expect normal, uncomplicated births may wish to share the experience with their children. Your child's age and emotional development will weigh heavily in your decision about whether or not to have him or her present at the birth.

If you want to explore this option, ask your child only after you are certain you'll be comfortable with it and that your doctor/midwife/doula is also, and that you'll be at a location (check your medical insurance here too) that can accommodate all those you expect to share in the birthing event. Only 1% of all American births take place at home. Parents can check in their area for home birth midwives at Citizens for Midwifery at www.cfmidwifery.

Even very young ones may have a definite preference about wanting to attend or not. Many children are intrigued by pictures of developing fetuses but that doesn't mean they'll respond well or really wish to be at a birth scene. Be sure to make it clear that your child can change his or her mind at any time.

Some do not believe children should be present at a birth; they feel the experience may be too traumatic. Many discourage allowing children under 4 to participate. They say the mother may be so concerned about the child that she won't be able to concentrate properly on the birth process.

In the March 1987 Journal of the American Academy of Child and Adolescent Psychiatry, a study reported that siblings in the delivery room may feel more anxiety than is realized by their parents. To the parents' surprise, most of the youngsters felt anxious about seeing the birth. Children under age 5 didn't know what to expect despite advance coaching. Often it was a case of the child wishing to be near mom rather than at the birth.

On the pro-side of the controversy, other parents feel that the experience will not be frightening to a child if it's handled properly. They believe participation in a birth gives a child a deep appreciation of childbirth and of life itself, and promotes the feeling of family. Some believe that sibling rivalry will be reduced and sibling bond will be stronger because of the child's presence in the birthing room.

In a study of fifty-five home births in Salt Lake City almost one-third of the mothers felt that sibling rivalry was reduced because of immediate contact with the newborn. Another study of forty children at a California birth center concluded that for some families sibling participation is valid, for others, it's not. Children who are ill or have had a recent traumatic experience relating to their own body or have had to cope with doctors and hospitals are not good candidates to be at a sibling's birth.

My four children (the youngest is 6) were present at the birth of our last baby. It made the baby seem more like part of the family to them, rather than an intruder, and I think it limited jealousy among the children.   Karen Gromada, Cincinnati, OH

Preparing a Child to be Present at the Birth

• Take the child with you for a prenatal visit at least once. Let the child meet the doctor or midwife and listen to the baby's heartbeat and see the ultrasound.

• Enroll the child in a class designed to prepare children for watching a birth, if one is available to you. Birth centers and hospitals with birthing rooms usually offer some sort of training appropriate to children of different ages. Remember to tell a child that going to the hospital doesn't mean anything is wrong with Mom.

• It's important to work with a maternity staff that won't mind a child being present at the birth.

• Some families never leave home for their birth. The midwife or doctor comes to them. Your older child will meet the midwife in her home office and at your home visits. When the midwife comes for the birth, the child knows this will be the night their new brother or sister will be born.

• Be sure the child understands all aspects of birth, including contractions and pain, the mother's red face, the sounds she may make, the breaking of the bag of waters, the possible episiotomy, blood that will be present on the mother and the baby (this is "extra blood" that mother doesn't need) and about the appearance of the placenta. Explain that cutting the umbilical cord does not hurt the baby, just as cutting hair and nails does not hurt. Prepare your child for the appearance of a newborn—naked, with bluish colored skin covered by the white lubricant.

• Use books, pictures, and videos to help with your explanations, including any pictures you have of your older child's birth or newborn period. ***Welcome With Love*** by Jenni Overend (Kane/Miller) is a children's book about a homebirth.

• Show a child how just one drop of red food coloring can make a whole glass of water red. This can help them understand that all the 'red stuff' they see is not mom loosing lots of blood.

• Tell your child that the baby will probably cry, and that he or she will not be able to play with the baby immediately after it is born, though it might be possible to let your child place a finger into the new baby's hand to "hold hands" shortly after the birth.

• Play "birth" just like you play "house."

> *Around the time I was seven and one-half months pregnant, we purchased an inexpensive fetoscope, and listening to the baby's "heartbeep" became part of our bedtime ritual. The one thing we forgot to mention was that the umbilical cord would have to be cut. It wasn't a big thing for Lisa, but we had forgotten to mention it and she asked a lot of questions about the cord.*
>
> *Kathy Parks, Boblingen, W. Germany*

• It's important for both parents to share the desire for the older child to attend the birth of the baby and that the child is interested in attending the birth without you having to do a hard sell.

• Prepare your child (and possibly yourself) for seeing you naked by bathing together and letting him or her see you dress and undress.

• Simulate for your child the positions and your facial expressions that may be seen during the birth and also the sounds you may make. Let kids know labor is hard work!

• Let the child see and touch the equipment you assemble for a home birth and explain the uses of the clamp, scissors, suction pump, and other items, as simply as you can.

• Mention the possibility of problems and explain that if they occur, the child will leave and the mother may go to the hospital labor room or surgical suite.

• Select one person (not the father) to be with the child throughout the entire birth process—someone who will have no responsibility for the mother or any part of the birth. This friend or relative should have a calm personality and will attend to the child's wants and needs, and take him or her from the room if necessary or desired. It's advisable for the person to attend classes with the child or at least to read some of the birthing books with him or her. Choose someone who will be able to concentrate on the child throughout, and who won't get wrapped up in the excitement of the delivery and forget about the child's needs. Be sure the child understands this arrangement. That person can also encourage the child to let mom know mom is doing a good job!

• Explain to your child beforehand that if asked to leave the room by mom or dad, it is not because the child is being rejected or that mom or dad are angry, but that there are some times when mom may need time-out or time alone.

In the Birthing Room

It is said that a child never asks to return the new baby "to the store or the hospital" where children often imagine they were 'bought.' They see for themselves that this baby is every bit as much a part of their family as they are.

• Be sure there are books, toys, games, and snacks for your child to enjoy during the "boring" times. A long labor will seem endless to a child. Keeping a child occupied until mom is ready to push is the job of the child's caretaker—not mom or dad.

• A small child can be upset by the temporary unavailability of mom during a contraction. Before responding look away and wait a few seconds before responding by saying, "Whew, I was having a contractiction. Now can I help you?"

• Let the child know that he or she can leave the room at any time and may or may not come back, as he or she chooses. Of course, the child's caretaker remains with the child and will need to have ideas of where to go (cafeteria, nursery, waiting room, lobby, a nearby park or store).

• Let your child help mom by holding ice chips, getting her a drink, rubbing her back, or walking around the room with her. An older child can be in charge of changing records/tapes/CDs and may even be allowed to take pictures or videos of the birth.

Don't be disappointed in your child's actions or reactions in a birthing room. Remember that children cannot "fail" in any way when attending their sibling's birth, the same way that mom and her partner do not fail at giving birth, no matter how the delivery goes.

If you're unsure about your child's presence at the birth, you might consider just having him or her nearby and brought into the birthing room immediately after the birth.

The Birth Doula and the Second Baby

First time parents can sometimes have a more romantic notion of what birth might be compared to the work it usually is. More second time parents are preparing for birth by bringing along a woman trained to give emotional support, practical information and comforting techniques throughout labor. Historically in almost every culture women have other knowledgeable women with them to soothe their efforts of the transition into motherhood or motherhood again.

Today this person has been given the name *doula* (doo-la), a Greek word for 'a woman's female servant.' For 25 years, medical research has shown that having a non-medical female, support person with the mother throughout her labor reduces the time of labor, reduces complication of labor and birth, and improves a woman's overall experience. For mom this can be a more satisfying birth and having a greater sense of her baby with more time spent holding, touching and talking to her newborn. These mothers are said to have less postpartum depression or anxiety.

Information about doulas can be found at Doulas of North America (DONA) www.DONA.org or toll free at 1-888-788-3662.

CHAPTER FOUR

How Can I Keep Our Older Child from Feeling Left Out?

Now your family is experiencing growing pains. You enjoy the feeling of competence you didn't have the first time, and you're not quite as frightened at the thought of your responsibility to the new little life, but as a mother, you're finding that there's just no way you can fully satisfy the needs of everyone. It's hard, sometimes impossible, to find time for those important private moments with your older child and with your husband or partner. Having two (or more) children definitely means more work for you.

All you can do is your best. Time is on your side. Patience, a good sense of humor, and plenty of love will see you through. It's important to realize that kids are very adaptable. Chances are your older child is not going to suffer or carry scars from this experience, especially if you make the effort to include him or her in every phase of your adjustment to a new kind of family life. With each additional child, your family changes, and changes are seldom easy. Don't assume the child will feel instant warmth or love for the baby, and don't be too disappointed if it doesn't happen. That's asking for too much too soon. Jealousy toward a new sibling is almost universal. Don't discourage your child's invention of an imaginary playmate if it occurs at this time. Instead, appreciate it! And don't pick this particular time to try to break a pacifier or security blanket habit, either.

> _Don't worry yourself sick over the transition for children at home. I drained myself mentally the first few days, then realized that I was the one having a rough time adjusting. I always wanted to be saying and doing the rights things—and no mom is perfect. Feel successful about your busy days if you have spent a little special time with each child._
>
> _Vicki Pouchet, Kalamazoo, MI_

Announcing the New Arrival

• Let the child help make the phone calls to announce the baby's arrival. Your child can even be the one to make the call to the grandparents announcing the news.

• Get treats for your child to pass around to friends and neighbors. You may be able to find some with "It's a boy/girl!" printed on the wrappers, or just tie pink or blue ribbons around whatever you give out.

• Give your older child a t-shirt bearing the message: "I'm the Big Brother/Big Sister." (See page 5 for additional 'messages.') You can probably also have one made up to your specs at a local t-shirt shop or quick print center. Or use fabric paint to make your own. (You can also order one in children's sizes from the back page of this book, if you wish.)

A Gift for the Older Sibling

• You may want to give your older child one super-present to help celebrate the birth—something that shows he or she is bigger and older, such as a riding toy for a toddler, or some rather sophisticated art materials for a preschooler.

• Tell your child it's a gift from the baby, perhaps spinning a story about how the new baby asked mom and dad to bring this specific gift to the baby's older brother or sister. A child who is old enough to understand the baby couldn't possibly "tell" the parents what to buy will still be delighted with the fanciful tale.

Within the Family

• Recognize the fact that you may find yourself enjoying the baby and snapping at your chatterbox toddler—almost wishing he or she would go away. Don't feel guilty! It's very normal. Some parents report just the opposite problem: the baby seems boring compared to the toddler who can do so many interesting things.

• Try to keep your older child's daily routine as normal as possible. Help your child understand the baby is not going to take over.

Have You Said to Your Child Lately...
"I love you."
"I'm glad (_the baby's name_) has you for a sister/brother!"
"You are my favorite 2- (or whatever age) year-old."
(_Inappropriate if older child is a twin!_)

• Remember to take as many pictures of the child as you do of the baby, and your older child should be alone in some of them. (But do remember to take many pictures of this second child, the one seen but fleetingly in family albums. One second child was convinced that she was adopted because there was no baby book for her, and few baby pictures in the family albums.)

• Make a point of having dad or mom talk to the older child first when arriving home, and then look in on the baby.

• Say, "My hands are busy right now" when your child wants attention and you're occupied with the baby. It's a little less personal than saying you're busy, and it may pacify the child.

• Give plenty of praise and recognition for good behavior and help.

• Try to juggle the baby's first and last feedings of the day so both children don't go to bed and get up at the same time. (Easier said than done!) Some parents are able to have breakfast alone with the older child before the baby wakes or when the baby naps after a 1st feeding.

• Schedule private time with your older child on occasion. If you can, get a sitter or leave the baby with your spouse so that you can do things with your older child that the baby can't do.

• Likewise, spend time alone with the baby, too. Your older child will have to learn to share you.

• Point out that babies have heard their sister or brother's voice when inside the uterus and now they want to see their face.

• If your family celebrates big events by planting a tree or with some other symbolic gesture, be sure the older child helps—and be sure to point out how his or her birth was celebrated in the same or a personalized way.

• When an activity is interrupted by the new baby, let your older child know you must attend to the baby but that you will be back and you will finish what you were doing together.

After Ben's birth, Nathan went through a stage during which he liked to whisper "secrets" in our ears. We would whisper back such things as, "Pssst, you sure have a nice baby." He thought that was great fun. 3-year-old Nathan still considers Benjamin his baby.

Carol Reinhard, Corvallis, OR

Our 3-1/2-year-old has had many imaginary playmates. They seem to change as her needs change. Since the birth of our last baby, she has a "big brother" and a big sister." They give her attention when I'm busy.

Sarah Holback, Albers, IL

Our 3-year-old went through a very clingy stage right before the baby arrived, and I feared the worst. But when our new son was born, things went much more smoothly than I had anticipated. He was very whiny and weepy for a few days after I returned from the hospital, but the baby seemed to be exactly what he expected and he quickly perked up. The world hadn't come to an end and soon he was noticing positive things about the baby on his own.

N. Warren, Columbus, OH

• Get a pet, if you can handle it. Even a goldfish will give your child something else to focus on. (On the other hand, if your oldest is under the age of 3 you may find yourself protecting the pet as well as the new baby from the affections of your older child.)

Teaching How to Hold A Baby

A little guidance will go a long way here.

• Explain and show how a baby should be held and that the head and neck need support.

• Use a soft chair with arms, a couch or a place in the middle of a bed for your older child to safely hold the baby.

• Stay near by to offer help and encouragement.

• Take a photo of the two together. If the baby starts to cry, explain it is not because of anything he or she did. Babies usually cry to let everyone know they are hungry, need a diaper change or just wish to be moved to another position.

• Praise your child for doing such a good job holding the new baby.

While You're Feeding the Baby

Be aware that your child of preschool age or younger is very apt to feel left out at feeding time and may feel a loss of intimacy. The child is also likely to feel particularly jealous at this time. But children also learn from this example of caring for others which will serve them well in their future.

• Make feeding "safer" if your older child is still little by bringing both the baby and the toddler into a room where you can close the door or put a gate across the doorway.

• Make careful preparations before you start feeding the baby. Set up a table, lay out a snack for the older child, and get out the toys and books you and the child will share while you feed the baby. Change toys regularly to maintain your child's interest. Ask your older child to pick out a book to read.

• Seat yourself on the couch so you and your older child can cuddle, read, or watch TV while you're feeding the baby. An older child can hold the book and turn the pages while you read and feed the baby

• Or sit on the floor with your child, where you can help with puzzles, games, and the like. Let your child draw or color at a nearby table.

• If your child is too young to answer the phone for you, a cordless phone would be a good investment. You won't have to jump up and answer it or let it go unanswered. Or just keep your cell phone in your pocket.

• Watch favorite TV shows or DVDs/videos together while feeding the baby.

• Tell stories to your older child about what he or she was like as a newborn while feeding the baby. Also talk about what the baby will be taught by this older brother or sister—smiling, walking and building with blocks.

Nursing

The intimacy of breastfeeding is difficult for an older child to accept when you yourself don't view it as a normal and natural part of baby care. You need to be relaxed at feeding time, especially if you're nursing. To calm yourself, use relaxation tips learned in childbirth classes or listen to soothing music while you nurse. Do your breathing exercises before nursing to help you relax and make the milk come down faster. Have your toddler or preschooler do them with you. Don't let yourself get angry with your older children's behavior or it may slow down your milk flow. Learn to stay calm and keep your priorities in order. Don't issue restrictions unless they are safety-related.

• Sometimes an older child is interested in trying nursing again. If you're comfortable with it (but only if you are), let your child try. Chances are it will be a quick, somewhat embarrassed attempt. The child probably won't like the taste of your milk, won't be able to suck properly, and will lose interest quickly.

• If an older child is complaining abut the amount of time nursing the baby takes, acknowledge that babies do take a lot of time and that you gave the same amount of time when he or she was a baby.

• Remember that breastfeeding has an added plus—you have an extra hand free to use with your older child. You can read or even cuddle your older child.

• When possible, let dad or another family member spend some time with the older child while you're nursing the baby.

Bottle-Feeding

• Let your child help you hold the baby's bottle. Explain how liquid must cover the nipple area so the baby won't swallow air.

• Hold your baby when bottle-feeding, but on occasion you may put the baby in an infant seat so you can play with the older child and still maintain eye contact with the baby.

• Let your child bottle-feed a doll with a realistic toy bottle. Look for one that seems to empty when it's inverted. When the child "feeds" the doll, it looks like the doll is really drinking the pretend milk.

• Babies are not as fussy as moms are about have formula or milk warmed up. If it makes your life less stressful to avoid this step, consider eliminating it.

When Visitors Come

• Stall visitors who come to see the new baby and let the older child be the center of attention for a few minutes. Remind them (but not in front of the older child) that the older sibling needs attention too.

• Have your child first invite visiting family and friends to wash their hands before holding the newborn. It will help keep germs at bay.

• Let your child lead the guests to the baby's room or help you bring the baby out, and maybe also help with serving refreshments.

• And, while refreshments are being eaten, don't be surprised if your child tells the visitors just how the baby gets his or her refreshments from inside Mommy's blouse.

• Show pictures of both the older child and the baby.

• Ask the child to unwrap the presents brought for the baby.

• Keep a supply of little gifts on hand to give the older child if visitors don't bring something.

• Or as some parents prefer to do, explain to children that babies "come with nothing" and need lots of things and that when their birthday comes, the presents will be only for them.

After making certain that my 3-1/2-year-old was safely occupied, I sat down to "quietly" nurse her new brother. All went quite well and I was congratulating myself on my abilities as a mom when a little voice came from the stairway: "Mom, could you come get my gum off the wall?" Oh well, at least she doesn't hit him.

Kathleen Bricker, Ann Arbor, MI

The Shared Room

Many American parents feel that children should have their own rooms, separate from their siblings, that each child needs the privacy and space offered by a room of one's own. That's not the norm in many other countries. In fact, a lot of parents here are now opting to put their kids together, even if they don't have to. And kids don't always object. As one child put it, "You and Dad share a room. Why do I have to be alone?"

Many parents feel that since bunking together with their sibling(s) was good enough for them—it's good enough for their kids.

The Wall Street Journal reported in October of 2004 that even affluent parents in large homes are having children share a bedroom in the belief that it will instill character. This 'kid-consolidation' plan is done in the interest of the no-spoiling school of child-rearing.

If your baby is going to share a room with a toddler you may want to keep the baby in your room for the first few weeks. Be cautious about a shared room with a child under the age of 3. Jealous and abusive behavior could possibly occur in early hours when you are not yet awake. This is one good reason to keep a baby monitor turned on in their bedroom as an extra check.

Other reasons for keeping the baby in your room in a bassinet or carriage initially are that the older child won't be disturbed. You also won't be taking a chance of the older one trying to pick up the baby, and you'll save yourself some running. On the other hand, the sooner you put the children together, the sooner they'll adjust.

• Don't ask for permission from your child—just announce it.

• Put the crib up in the shared room a few weeks before the baby arrives to set up the scenario of the shared room.

• If the child is jealous because the baby is in your room, set up a corner of another room where the bassinet can be placed until your own bedtime.

• Consider adopting the "family bed" plan on occasion, if it's not against your inclinations. One way to stretch the space in the parents' bed is to put a bassinet or crib (with one side removed) right next to the bed.

• Room-sharing by siblings should begin once your infant sleeps through the night.

• Provide privacy in a shared room, especially if the kids are older, by setting up a screen or room divider of some kind. Bookshelves work well. You can attach blinds to tracks on the ceiling and floor to make a more permanent separation. Or even build four- or five-foot plywood walls in a corner of the room. Pad the walls to muffle noise, and cover the padding with fabric attached with a staple gun. Keep in mind that there will still be some sibling fighting.

• Try to provide play or study space for your older child in another part of the house so the schedules of the two children won't conflict. At the very least, a child should have a special possessions space or box that the younger child should not have access to.

• Let your baby nap in your bedroom so the older child can use their bedroom for play during baby's nap time.

• Keep a baby monitor (intercom) in the children's bedroom to hear when the baby is awakening. You can then get to the baby before the older child is disturbed.

• Put the child who sleeps soundest to bed first.

Some parents make very few accommodations and still find that their children adjust. Babies get used to sleeping anywhere and toddlers learn to sleep through wakenings and diaper changes.

In the book, _THE FAMILY BED_ by Tine Thevenin, the author discusses how children who grow up in a "family bed" often wean themselves from sleeping with the parents by sleeping with siblings. Here children not only share a room but also share a bed! Separate rooms for different gender children usually occurs around age 5.

Childproofing the Shared Room

• Take every precaution you can to protect the baby from the attention of your toddler, even loving, well intentioned ones. Set the crib mattress at its lowest point and leave the crib side up at all times.

• Remove any furniture (such as stools) that the sibling could use to climb into the crib.

• Try to get the baby up in the morning before the older child wakes, or put down at night after the older one is asleep. And try to keep afternoon nap times separate.

• Put away, for a time, toys with small parts that your older child might try to share with the baby. At least keep such toys in another part of the house. Give the older sibling a closed container (such as a tackle box) for such items.

• Later, when the baby is mobile and curious, give your older child a feeling of control by perhaps supplying locks for a few drawers in which precious and/or dangerous objects can be kept.

• Create private play space by carpeting a closet you can spare. and maybe even removing the door(s).

A Sibling Library

Books can help prepare a child for life with a new sibling. They describe feelings that children can come to understand are normal and they provide expectations of life with a new baby.

Use your child's name instead of the one assigned by the book, if you think the story will be enhanced by this tip.

There are many, many such sibling preparation books available. Even I've written one—*A New Baby at KoKo Bear's House.* Here a delightful unisex bear goes through the family's stages of pregnancy and birth. KoKo feels bad when the gift from Aunt Beartrice is for the new baby. But in the end it is KoKo who 'teaches' the baby to smile.

Here are desciptions of several other titles to get you started. Just visiting the library or children's bookstore you will find these and certainly many others. You can search an online bookstore by just typing in "Baby Brother" or "Baby Sister" or "New Sibling" and long lists will present themselves.

Books for a Younger Child (ages 2-5)

The Berenstain Bears' New Baby by Stan & Jan Berenstain.
Small Bear has outgrown his snug little bed. Papa builds him a new one just in time for the arrival of his new baby sister and he proudly stretches out in his new, bigger bed.

What to Expect When the New Baby Comes Home by Heidi Murkoff.
With the help of Angus, the loveable Answer Dog, kids learn what babies do and don't do and what having one around the house will be like.

The New Baby by Fred Rogers.
In this full color, photo book, simple, reassuring captions talk about different feelings and happenings that occur when a new baby enters a family. The photos show various siblings rather than just one child's point of view.

The New Baby at Your House by Joanna Cole.
Lovely color photographs of a variety of different families and siblings record the arrival of a new baby. The text is supportive and reassuring for new brothers and sisters, describing in honest, positive terms what life is like when a new baby joins the family.

Za-Za's Baby Brother by Lucy Cousins.
Daughter Za-Za gets little attention from her parents until the baby goes to sleep and she then gets the hugs she needs.

Geraldine's Baby Brother by Holly Keller.
Geraldine, a lovable piglet wanted a baby brother, but not "that" one.

I'm a Big Sister and *I'm a Big Brother* by Joanna Cole.
A male and female version of having a new baby at home and how to inspire good behavior plus notes for parents.

Spot's Baby Sister by Eric Hill.
This board book (with lift-the-flaps) has Spot showing his sister Suzi to his friends.

The Baby by John Burningham.
In this sweet, 24-page book, a big brother finds that sometimes he likes the baby and sometimes he doesn't.

Here Come the Babies by C. & L. Anholt.
In rhyming verses, a toddler's mischievous relationship with her baby brother is featured.

Mommy's Lap by Ruth Horowitz & H. Sorensen.
Sister Sophie feels that this new baby takes up all the room on Mommy's lap, even before he is born.

Mommy's in the Hospital Having a Baby by Maxine Rosenberg.
Photos by Robert Maas "takes" kids on a visit to the hospital where it covers everything but the actual delivery.

Julius, The Baby of the World by Kevin Henkes.
Lilly was the best big sister mouse in the world, before brother Julius was born. Then it was a different story.

The Baby Sister by Tommy dePaola.
DePaola's illustrations are warm and affectionate as he remembers his past and the arrival of his baby sister.

When I am a Sister by Robin Ballard.
An older sister thinks about what her step-mom's having a new baby will mean to her life when she sees them all the next year.

Mom's Home by Jan Ormerod.
In this nearly wordless book, a pregnant mother takes time out to share a private moment with her toddler.

Welcome, Little Baby by Aliki. This is a picture book done with a warm, delicate artistic touch, showing a baby doing typical things.

Baby Says by John Steptoe.
This book is often considered a multicultural book because the children in the book are African-American, though ethnicity is not at all the subject of this story. Toddlers (and siblings of toddlers) of any ethnicity will relate to this simple story about the warmth of a sibling relationship.

Books for a Little Older Child

Sharing by Nanette Newman.
Amy is worried that her new baby brother will monopolize her parents' time.

101 Things To Do With a New Baby by Jan Ormerod.
A 32-page picture book written from the view of a six year old sister about her baby sibling and their daily activities.

Big Like Me by Anna Grossnickle Hines. "I'm going to show you everything," says the big brother to his new sibling. And, indeed, he is the perfect guide for the child's first year.

A Baby Sister for Frances by Russell & Lillian Hoban.
Frances is a badger who decides to run away because everyone is busy looking after the baby. She doesn't run very far, and soon discovers that living by herself isn't so nice after all.

When the New Baby Comes, I'm Moving Out by Martha Alexander.
Oliver decides he'll leave home when the new baby arrives, but after a talk with Mom he thinks it might be okay to stay and be a big brother.

Nobody Asked Me if I Wanted a Baby Sister by Martha Alexander.
The baby has arrived and Oliver tries to get rid of her, until a clever girl makes him feel loved and wanted by his new sister.

I'll Fix Anthony by Judith Viorst.
A little brother thinks of ways to someday get revenge on his older brother.

Arthur's Baby by Marc Brown.
Arthur becomes a resident babysitter as he confronts the trials and tribulations of having a new sister.

Angel's Mother's Baby by Judy Delton.
Angel, who has an older brother, learns that her mother is having a baby. Suddenly everything is more complicated for this soon-to-be middle child.

My New Baby & Me: A First Year Record Book for Big Brothers & Sisters by Dian G. Smith
A beautiful, large format, quality paperback, this colorful and classy book has spaces for filling in "my" baby's development and offers a cooperative venture for parents and older siblings and insures that the second baby's history is recorded.

Turning on to Sibling Video

Here are VHS video guides for brothers and sisters of new babies. Check with your library or go to www.Amazon.com to order.

Growing Up Well - Hey, What About Me?
This is a delightful 25 minute video created for 2- to 6-year-olds showing real siblings with babies that kids can identify with. The kids on camera are fun to watch. The video features games, lullabies and bouncing rhymes to do with babies. Feelings of anger and loneliness are handled nicely.

Oh Baby! / Those Baby Blues
This is a live action video featuring Gus, a streetwise English Bulldog who believes that babies ruin perfectly good families. Through Gus's eyes children learn what to expect and that their feelings are like everyone else's. 'Those Baby Blues' is an informational video for parents of new siblings featuring two childcare experts.

Sesame Street - A New Baby in My House
Live-action Sesame Street characters help an older sibling adjust to a new (but not a newborn) sibling. When little Alice breaks something, Snuffy realizes it's not always easy for brothers and sisters to get along. Mrs. Snuffle helps Snuffy feel better with a story she reads to him. There are 6 musical numbers. It comes with a parent's guide to address issues of sibling rivalry.

CHAPTER FIVE

How can I Get Our Jealous Older Child to Accept (or even like!) the Baby?

Your first child has had you all to himself or herself (as none of your children ever will), so it's not surprising if some negative feelings toward the "intruder" develop. The experience of having a sibling thrust on one has been likened to that of a wife whose husband brings home a second spouse, saying, "I love you so much that I want another one like you."

Research indicates that a child's personality has the most effect on how they react to a new baby, says Kifa Royce, RN, from the University of Michigan Health System. Also, children with a close relationship with their father seem to adjust better. Stress on the family can also affect a child's adjustment.

It's best to follow your older child's lead, letting the sibling relationship develop at its own pace. While it's not unusual for an older child to hang over an infant, fascinated with every detail, it's also normal for a sibling to show only minimal interest or even hostility. Neither attitude predicts the future relationship.

Wise parents don't ignore jealousy, and they don't panic if they see it developing. They acknowledge it, letting the child know it's all right to have such feelings. They're understanding and patient, but they do not let the child dictate the household rules. Remember that you're the grown-up. Discipline when necessary, lay down your rules, and don't explain everything a dozen times. Still, five minutes of your time when a child needs it can be more beneficial than an hour when it's convenient for you. Be consistant.

The best way to deal with problem behavior is to provide some one-on-one time with your older child. Children want your attention if they are having a hard time adjusting and negative attention beats no attention at all. As hard as it is, try to make some special time for that new big brother or sister when there will be no interruptions. If necessary, take your phone off the hook for ten or twenty minutes while you devote yourself exclusively to your child.

Love Can Be Shared

Show your older child in a lovely and concrete way, how your love can be shared with the new baby without being lessened for him or her.

Set out three candles. The first represents mom and dad, the second is the older child, and the third is the new baby. Light the first candle. The flame represents love. With the first candle, light the second, and then the third. Like the flames, the love is separate, yet equal, for all. Lighting the third candle in no way diminishes the flame of the second.

Above all, don't try to equate "fair" with "equal." Your older child must understand from the beginning, that the one who needs the most attention will get it—and that right now, the baby is going to need the most. But don't try to be so fair with your attention that you leave out someone important—yourself!

Sometimes a child is afraid to show these natural feelings of jealousy, fearing a loss of the parents love. All siblings will feel some jealousy, and all siblings need the chance to express their feelings and have them recognized.

Let your older child know how much you love having an older child, too.

Jealousy in a Child 2 or Under

The younger a child is, the less ready he or she will be to share and enjoy the new baby. A toddler this age has held the firm belief that parents exist for him or her alone. Now that belief has been shattered. It's a fine point, but some experts say that what a child this age feels is more envy than jealousy; he or she envies the attention the baby is getting.

The older child needs careful watching; a "conscience" is not yet developed and it won't bother the child in the least to hurt the baby. His or her thought may be, "take the baby back—get rid of it!" whether or not the thought can be put into words. A child needs understanding. Your response, expressed without threats, should be, "You don't have to like the baby, but you may not hurt the baby!"

> *I had to wheel my newborn from room to room in a buggy to protect him from my 2-year-old. (You would have had to know my 2-year-old to understand why!)* Jill Heasley, Fresno, CA

Jealousy in a 3-Year-Old

Your 3-year-old can suffer from two conflicting responses to having a sibling: the desire to be a baby, small and weak and cared for, and the desire to be big and strong and independent. The child may swing between regression (resuming habits long outgrown) and anger about having some independence thwarted by the new baby's needs and demands.

Your child may be angry at you for being "dethroned," and may even refuse to talk to you sometimes. He or she may also be wary of showing anger for fear of losing you altogether, being "extra good" and denying feelings and turning them inward. He or she may know better by now, but still take out that anger on the baby with too-hard pats or squeezes and surreptitious pinches. Be aware that the anger may also be taken out on the family pet, in observance of the pecking order.

Jealousy in a 4- or 5-Year-Old

Your preschooler, capable now of exercising self-control and understanding fully that the baby is here to stay, may have the feeling that he or she is unloved and re-jected by you. The child wants to be grown-up and may demonstrate this by a lot of "watch me, see how big/strong/clever I am" activities and other thinly disguised bids for attention. He or she doesn't want to share parents with an infant that does "disgusting things" and takes up so much time.

The child may be very jealous of attention that the same-sex parent gives the baby and may compensate by focusing on the opposite-sex parent, i.e. if Suzi has lost Mom's undivided attention, Daddy belongs to her. Or a child may single out a grandparent or special adult friend for a possessive relationship.

Disappointment may be another of the child's emotions—the baby is the wrong sex, can't do anything, and is just a nuisance. Don't worry about giving the child ideas when you make statements about his or her feelings, such as "You wish you were the only one again," or "You don't like me having to spend so much time with the baby, do you?" The feelings are there, and talking about them should help. Try creating a "family" of sock dolls to help your child verbalize feelings about family roles.

Jealousy in School-Age Children

Your school-age child may show some of the reactions of a preschooler, appearing to be at ease with the baby while holding back real feelings or showing exaggerated and insincere affection for the infant. This child, however, has interests of his or her own and capabilities that are obviously far superior to those of the baby. He or she may be jealous and somewhat resentful, but may also be proud to have a baby in the family, something that makes him or her a bit of a celebrity with peers in the neighborhood and at school.

Jealousy in Preteens and Teens

Your preteen or teenager is unlikely to have feelings of jealousy or resentment; his or her life is full and busy. Some kids this age do feel a bit embarrassed that their "old" parents have reproduced. A girl this age might be afraid that people will think the baby is hers if she's seen caring for the infant. Most of these older kids, though, look on the baby as a joy, an amusing and lovable live plaything. Later on, when the baby becomes a toddler and gets into their things, their attitude may change.

> *I think our 3-1/2-year-old is back talking us mainly because of jealousy of a little brother who moves around in her territory now. A lot of love and setting a good example are important, though they haven't solved our problem.*
>
> Nancy Loge, Wilmar, MN

While studies and experience teach us that violence between siblings is the most frequent type of aggression in our society, it should help you to know that it is not based on the fear of losing a parent's affection or favors as children get older.

Research by Richard Felson at the State University of New York (Albany) suggests that sibling rivalry is more mundane than psychological. It evolves around competition over use and acquisition (not ownership) of "stuff." By teen years, closeness in age and sex are minimal factors.

The way parents intervene in kids' squabbles either reduces competition or makes it worse. Parents' mediation in fights appears to increase aggression. In other words, kids were more willing to fight when they could count on their parents interference. Parents, it seems, have a better chance of achieving peace when they work on house rules and parameters that prevent them from playing referee.

Helping Children Handle Their Feelings of Jealousy

• Sometimes "babying" a child who craves it can help the adjustment.

• Admit to your child that the baby can be a nuisance; you can express your own occasional annoyance, but don't ever apologize for the baby's existence.

• Let your baby "wait" once in a while when you're finishing up something with your older child.

• Give your older child new privileges—a later bedtime, increased allowance, special activities—now that he or she is a big brother or big sister. This may be the time to start letting a preschooler play outdoors alone—a great "grown-up" activity—if circumstances are just right.

• Be sensitive if your child doesn't particularly like the role of big brother or sister thrust upon him or her. "Yes, sometimes it's hard to be the big brother/sister."

• Provide some out-of-home experiences for a young child. Your 2- or 3-year-old may enjoy a regular play group, or a special personal experience like going to the zoo with a babysitter. This should not be done, however, if you are just trying to get the child out of the way, or if the child interprets the event as such.

• Don't make your child feel guilty about feeling jealous. He or she can't control these feelings.

• Don't tell your child how to feel. Let your child tell you how he or she feels and acknowledge those feelings. "I hear you're feeling unhappy about the baby."

• Point out the fact that someday he or she might be a mother or father, too, and may have an older child and a baby, just as you do.

> *Be patient. Our 3-year-old was quite jealous when our little girl was born. We let her help out as much as possible. A year later, they are the best of friends.*
> *Chris Rohret, Tiffin, IA*

• Stress how the baby loves or enjoys having an older brother or sister. "See how Jennifer smiles when she sees you. She thinks you are very special."

• Stagger naps and feedings so you can have some time alone with the older child.

• Look at old pictures together, especially those that show you doing the things with and for the older child that you now do for the baby.

• Let your child overhear you telling another adult how helpful and kind the older sibling is with the baby. Direct praise, unfortunately, can sometimes be perceived as a "con job" (which it may very well be).

• Say "I love you" often—without adding "and the baby, too."

• Let your child know it's normal to have happy, sad and jealous feelings when a new baby arrives in the family.

Second-Stage Jealousy: When the Baby Becomes Mobile

Right now, you're thinking only of the immediate acceptance of your new baby by your older child. Sibling rivalry does go on, though, sometimes into adulthood. You might as well accept the fact that you'll be reading, hearing, and talking about jealousy—and living with it—for a long time to come.

Once your infant is mobile, your concerns with sibling rivalry will focus on protecting the older child's possessions and "space," and, just as important, his or her place in the family.

• Teach your older child that the baby who grabs things can be easily distracted by a quick gift of something else. (A sibling under the age of 2 or even 3 may not comprehend this trick.)

• Don't make an issue out of sharing. Just give positive strokes for being able to engage in a wider range of play. The abstract concept of ownership and sharing are simply beyond the understanding of a 2- or 3-year-old.

• Explain that a baby who grabs (toys, hair, etc.) is simply exploring a new world and doesn't understand "mine vs. yours" or how his or her actions hurt others.

• Encourage the older child to minimize problems by keeping his or her things up high or safely put away.

• Provide locks and keys for boxes and drawers to help the older child protect precious belongings.

• Be sensitive to baby items and toys previously used by your older child being "passed down" to the baby. The older child might decide to reclaim an item to protect his or her status if feeling threatened.

• Get an extra baby gate for the door of your older child's room to keep the baby out.

• Continue to avoid focusing too much attention on the baby in the presence of the older child. If friends and relatives persist, draw attention to the older one's abilities and achievements in any way you can. Don't stress the *"Mother's helper with the baby"* aspect after the first few months.

• Go through your older child's toys and put away what isn't being played with. Bring them out later to share with the baby.

• Ask your older child to choose some toys from his or her collection for the baby to play with. A toddler often enjoys "taking control" of the baby's play. Another form of control may be shown by being overprotective of the baby or by becoming mom's 'best baby helper.'

> *Problems were insignificant until 9-month-old sister "got into her stuff." They fought then and two years later they're still fighting!*
>
> D. Schipani, Ellicott City, MD

• Be sure the older child gets a fair share of attention, love, and praise within the family circle, too.

• Make and observe a few house rules to ensure the physical safety of the younger child, but don't overprotect him or her. You'll be setting up a situation for resentment.

Regression in Young Children

Be aware that regressive behavior (a return to baby behavior) can occur after a week, a month, at seven months (most common), or even longer after the arrival of a second baby. It is normal. Don't punish it or you might reinforce the child's feelings about being bad or unwanted. Be patient, and don't overlook your child's needs at this trying time.

• Being a baby is, to a child, the key to getting a parent's attention, and regression seems to be a way to compete on the baby's own terms. Your child may be genuinely confused about why certain behavior (thumb sucking, wetting pants) is bad when he or she does it, and acceptable or even good when the baby does it.

• Be aware that a young child's return to babyish habits in such matters as toilet training, eating , dressing and baby talk may or may not be a sign of jealousy; it may simply reflect stress.

• Treat regressive behavior (especially if it's wetting or soiling pants) without punishment and using non-judgmental language. A return to diapers can be done matter-of-factly.

• Consider indulging regressive behavior to help a child work through it. Try changing his or her clothes on the changing table, even adding a sprinkle of baby powder; or serve your toddler milk or juice in a baby bottle.

• Don't scold or criticize your child. Instead, make an effort to show even more of your love and caring, telling the child how lucky the baby is to have such a nice big brother or sister.

• Praise generously any mature behavior you can spot, and point out the many advantages of being older and more grown-up.

• Encourage grandparents or other relatives to offer your regressing, older child special consideration and attention.

> *My 3-year-old son seemed to love his new little sister, but I guess I knew that I was kidding myself when he gave up walking for a few days and started to crawl again, just when she did.*
>
> *Roz Nemer, Minnetonka, MN*

• If your child is in daycare or nursery school, he or she is probably showing regressive behavior there, too. Consult with the caregiver or teacher about helping the child handle jealousy. Some schools have special celebrations to mark the transition to big-brother-or-sister status.

Behavioral Warning Signs

It is time to look into getting professional counseling when your child persistently:

- avoids or ignores the baby and is unable to show the baby any affection
- is consistently angry, taunting and aggressive towards the baby
- is overly good or caring with the baby yet still has nightmares and sleeping difficulty

---

Helping Your Child Handle Anger

Your older child may be angry—very angry—with you for bringing home this intruder. He or she may be afraid to show this anger, so you should watch carefully for signs of it. One 3-year-old thinly disguised his anger with what he thought was humor, calling his mother "the big nipple." Another made no such attempt and simply walked up to his mother and gave her a swift kick in the shin while she was nursing the baby.

Yet another family used a toy telephone to great advantage during this stage. The child used the telephone to express negative feelings about the baby: "Doctor, the baby is dying! Come and take him back to the hospital!" The telephone allowed the child to get the feelings out safely, because everyone was aware that it was all "just pretend." Give your toddler or preschooler as many opportunities as possible to vent anger in acceptable ways.

One caution: A toddler may handle a baby awkwardly and even hurt the child unintentionally. Be sure to distinguish between such accidental behavior and a deliberate attempt to cause pain.

• Encourage physical activity to work off anger—running around outside, punching a pillow or mattress, or throwing stones into a pond are just a few ways for a child to expend angry energy.

• Use a punching toy or stuffed animals that can be thrown around, hit, talked to, or punished by an angry child. Playing with a family of sock dolls (the child can help you sew or draw on facial features and expressions) can be a creative way for the child to demonstrate feelings of anger and frustration that he or she is unable to express verbally.

• State plainly that it's okay for the child to be angry with you—that you're angry with him or her sometimes, too—but that it is not okay to hit or kick mom or the baby. "We don't hurt anyone, no matter how we feel. I don't let anyone hurt you and I won't let anyone hurt your baby brother or sister, either."

"I Almost Had a Heart Attack"

Once I heard the baby make a strange noise. I turned around to see my 2-year-old standing on my 2-month-old baby's stomach! No permanent harm was done, but I almost had a heart attack!

Becky Wilkins, Lubbock, TX

Mother hears splash from bathroom, runs to investigate. There stands 2-1/2-year-old on the floor, 1-year-old with feet in toilet. 2-year-old, "He looked like he wanted to take a little swim!"

Kay Coburn-Dyer, Bloomington, MN

Our 3-year-old had developed a game with her father. She would "hide" under a pillow, and he would search for her. I came back from the door one day to find her holding the pillow over her 4-month-old sister's face as the little one struggled for breath. I overreacted and pushed her away. Finally, sobbing, she told me she had been teaching the baby to hide, not trying to hurt her.

P. M. Dash, Marietta, CA

One day when Rebecca was only a few weeks old, my 5-year-old son decided she should be sleeping on the couch. He plucked her from her bassinet and walked toward the couch. I entered the room, and my son—caught red-handed—decided to get rid of the evidence. He was too far from the bassinet, so he tossed her toward the sofa, about three feet away. It could only have been an act of God that Rebecca actually landed "safely"—still asleep!

Robyn Neuman, Beaver Dam, WI

• Use aggressive behavior directed at you (the parent) to help a child attach words to his or her negative behavior: "Are you angry with me because I gave the baby so much attention today? I can understand how you wouldn't feel good about that. What can you and I do special tonight (read a book) or tomorrow (go to the park)?"

• Teach your child to express anger verbally: "*I'm mad at you because_____*" and then talk about the feelings. Very young children can't do this effectively (they're better at tantrums) and some older children have a harder time with this technique than others.

• If you're a working mother on maternity leave, your older child is enjoying a bonus of your attention, but be aware that he or she may also be thinking, "She stays home for the baby, but not for me." A little discussion may be in order.

• Remind yourself, when your child is venting anger, it's better that the negative feelings come out rather than remain hidden.

"Big Kids" Can Help

• Let a toddler watch proceedings at the dressing table from a nearby stool, handing you items you need and helping pat the baby dry after a bath.

• Let the older child choose which (or just 2 or 3 choices) outfit the baby should wear.

• Wear an apron with big pockets to store baby accessories in, and take out just one at a time to avoid more help than you need.

• Let the child fetch and carry for you around the house, sort the baby's laundry, or help burp the baby.

• Let your child set the baby swing control in motion.

• Do put the baby safely in the infant seat inside a playyard or playpen if you leave the room even for a minute. And set the crib mattress at its lowest point so you won't get "help" in picking up the infant.

• Be aware that the baby's soft spot, at the top of the head, is protected by a firm muscle. Don't overreact when your child inadvertently (or maybe not inadvertently) touches that area, which you've just explained is delicate and to be avoided.

• Remember that a very young child's willingness to help may exceed his or her ability to do so. Both baby and child must be protected. Be available to supervise holding or feeding and don't entrust the baby to the child's care alone for any extended period of time.

• Accept help with the baby book and photo album from even a very young child; take advantage of the activity as an opportunity to talk about the older child's baby years.

• Let your older child help pick out baby food you may need for the baby in the grocery store and other items.

> _Don't be overprotective. Hovering over the baby with too many restrictions suggests inappropriate behavior. We let our son experiment, within reason, and learn for himself what his sister did and didn't like._
>
> Jodi Junge, Huntingdon Valley, CA

• Encourage the child to be a teacher by showing the baby (once past infancy) how to drink from a cup, to crawl, walk, draw, etc.

• Let an older child make up and record a message for the phone-answering machine: "Mom's busy with the baby; the best time to call is around four o'clock (or whenever)."

• Welcome the real help a preteen or teenager can give you, but try not to overdo your requests, possibly building resentment.

• Treat your babysitting older child with the same consideration you do an outsider, whether or not you pay for the service.

There is a tendency to expect a child to be more independent because he or she is older. If you expect less independence, you could be doing both your older child and yourself a favor.

> _I have to admit this was one area in which I failed miserably. I was so afraid of my 3-year-old hurting the baby, I discouraged togetherness. I wish I could have done it differently._
>
> Linda Merry, St. Louis Park, MN

Playing With the Baby

• Put your older child's finger in the baby's palm and show your own delight when the baby clenches it.

• Show your child how to test the baby's sucking reflex by putting the back of the child's hand on the baby's mouth or touching the baby's lower lip gently with a finger.

• Show the child how to get the baby to turn his or her head by having the child gently stroke one of the baby's cheeks or shake a rattle near the baby's head.

• Let your child join in the infant games you play with the baby, such as *Pat-a-Cake* and *This Little Piggy*. And explain that the baby will be interested in any game for only a few minutes at a time.

• Stimulate both children by exposing them to different odors, such as vanilla, peanut butter, and coffee. Enjoy the baby's reactions with your older child.

• Reinforce the baby's responsiveness to the older sibling. "Look how happy your baby brother becomes when you sing to him."

• Become the pretend-voice of the baby (a high pitched voice works well) and ask the older child questions on behalf of the baby or just chat. It can be a fun game.

Teaching Gentleness

• Start before the baby is born by encouraging your child to practice being gentle with your pet, a doll or stuffed animal. Use the doll to show your child how to hold a baby correctly, supporting the back and neck and you won't have to constantly correct your child when the baby arrives.

• Continue the practice by having the child hold and care for a doll while you do the same for the baby.

• Talk a lot about the need for gentleness, explaining that little babies "hurt easier" than big kids do.

• Be gentle yourself, with both children. Your example is always the best lesson.

• Speak calmly and quietly. Don't yell or shout, "Stop!" or "Careful!"—however much you may be tempted (and you will be tempted!).

• Reinforce the gentle behavior your older child does display. "I like how you hold your baby brother so gently," or "hold her hand gently, that's right."

• Make use of your family pet to help your child develop gentleness in playing with it. Stress the pet's value as a friend and companion—it may have to sit in for you occasionally!

How to Keep Kids Close

We want our kids to form strong and loving bonds that will carry into adulthood—even when we don't have these type of relations with our own siblings. This is our wish for our children—not theirs for themselves.

We can help set the stage but all efforts at fairness unfortunately will not insure this will happen. While it's important to try to be fair with your kids, that does not necessarily mean treating them the same—despite their protestations.

It is important to downplay behavior such as teasing and bullying. Even if it is not meant to be harmful, it can still be hurtful. And children can have very long memories. Also, having a 'favorite' child can be damaging to their relationship as well as yours with your children.

Children's relationships will change over the years and unfortunately you can not 'legislate' closeness. Ultimately their relationship will be more of a result of their personalities and life's events.

In retrospect, I found it was I who should have been better prepared. I perpetuated Brian's aggressive responses (hitting, ripping, breaking toys) by my own extreme concern for his hurt feelings. He sensed my sympathy and tested me beyond what was called for. I was so worried about him that I went so far as not to snuggle the baby when he was around.

Wendy Short, Bethel Park, PA

CHAPTER SIX

How Can I Help Our Child Handle Special Circumstances?

It's impossible to predict the special circumstances that may surround a birth, although some—an adoption or a cesarean birth—are known about in advance. If you do know what will be different, you can prepare your older child as best you can. Otherwise, you'll take what comes as a family—learning, adjusting, and, perhaps, grieving together.

If You're Adopting a Baby

• Familiarize your child with the details of reproduction and birth just as you would if you were giving birth. Be sure that he or she, especially if quite young, understands that the baby does not come out of nowhere and has been, or will be, born like any other baby.

• Pay special attention to actual or implied questions as to why you're making this special effort to add to your family. Having a baby is one thing; going out to search for a baby may be harder to explain and harder for your child to understand.

• Explain to the child old enough to ask, why a mother would not want her own baby—that the baby's parents couldn't provide it the proper love and care and knew it was best for the baby to have a loving family raise him or her. It never means that the child was unloved.

• Take advantage of any classes or information offered by your adoption agency that may help your child understand adoption.

• Let your child participate as fully as possible in the adoption procedures— looking at pictures of the baby, going with you to pick up the baby, and if your child is old enough, being present at legal proceedings.

• Study together the culture of a foreign-born adoptee, preparing your child as well as yourself for differences and for adjustments that you will all have to make.

• Celebrate the adoption just as you would a birth, including the extended family and friends. Let your older child participate as much as possible in arrangements for the celebration.

• Recognize that resentment expressed by your own child is to be expected (after the initial excitement and newness wears off), but may not necessarily be attributed to adoption. The process of being displaced by the new baby and having to share family affection is hard on any sibling. A normal response of "take the baby back" should be your cue to give extra, individual attention.

• Check with the NATIONAL ADOPTION INFORMATION CLEARINGHOUSE, 330 C Street SW, Washington, DC 20447, (703-352-3488 or 888-251-0075) *naic.acf.hhs.gov,* or email: naic@caliber.com for their information that helps family and sibling adjustment.

• And ADOPTIONSHOP.COM, 459 N. Gilbert Road #C-100, Gilbert, AZ 85234 (480-346-9187) *www.adoptionshop.com,* which has an extensive list of books for children that can be purchased on their site.

If the New Baby is a Half-Sibling

Each situation is different because of the variations possible, i.e. natural mother or stepmother having the new baby—age of the child and primary residence of the child. Regardless of the details, there are some things you can do to make the adjustment easier:

• Be aware that a child who may have been pleased with a parent's marriage and stepparent will not necessarily be thrilled with a new sibling. It's one thing to adjust to a stepmom or stepdad and quite another to add a new sibling. It's direct competition for affection!

• Try to see the situation from a child's viewpoint. It looks like there is only so much love to go around. While a child might have complete love from each natural parent in each separate household, the addition of a baby in one of those homes may be perceived by the child as having only half as much love available.

• It's true that an "ours" child can bring siblings from different households together because they now share a blood relative. But don't burden the new child with the responsibility of unifying the family, especially as that child gets older.

• Remember that a child moving between households can be influenced by the attitude of the other parent, who may not be thrilled (and may even be angry) about the new arrival.

• Let a child express the feelings that are pushing and pulling him or her. Don't judge or deny or say that he or she shouldn't feel that way. Feelings are real. Accept them as they are expressed and give them time to change.

• Do everything you can to help grandparents and other relatives accept the new baby as part of the extended family and to demonstrate their acceptance of the older half-siblings.

• Point out examples of half-siblings in families of friends and relatives. Older children may be surprised to find that they have lots of company in their situation.

• Remember this is one more change for a child who has already been through a lot of change. Don't be disappointed or surprised if the news of a new baby is met with less than a joyous response.

• Your child will probably have a lot of questions that he or she may not feel free to ask. Try to anticipate them and provide honest answers. (Will the family be moving—again—to make room for the baby? What will the baby's last name be? Is a half-sibling as good as a "whole" sibling? Will they like the baby better than they like me?)

• Be aware that if your child has been secretly hoping that his or her real parents will get back together, the presence of a baby may dash those hopes forever. This could be yet another reason for the child to resent (or even hate) the baby.

• If the stress of pregnancy or the new baby causes friction between you and your spouse, reassure your older child that it doesn't mean another divorce is imminent. In fact, your decision to have the baby can be evidence that you believe the marriage will last.

• Be prepared for the possibility that the new baby may also cause jealousy between parents. (Does he or she love this baby more than he or she loves my child?) Discuss these feelings openly and honestly with your spouse, and try not to involve your child, if possible.

> *When my visiting stepson's mother became pregnant, he was visibly upset— came around for lots of snuggles on the couch, and wanted (for the first time) to call me "Mom", turned a deaf ear on anything to do with babies. When his father's and my new baby was announced a year or so later, he took it all in stride. (P.S. He's just great with both little brothers now.)*
> *T. Burbank, New York, NY*

If You're Having Two (or More)

If you are expecting twins or your new arrival turns out to be two instead of one, be sure to seek out your local parents-of twins support group. You need the advice and support rights from the start, so don't waste any time getting it. Your doctor or a nurse at the hospital may be able to help you find a group, or check with the sources listed on the next page. With an older singleton at home, be aware that problems in trying to deal with the arrival of twins will be greater than if you brought home only one baby. Not only is the older child displaced—but by two, no less. Mother and Father are more tired and busy. Friends and family are even more intrigued by twins. It is very easy for an older child to get lost in those first few weeks and become resentful. If the twins are the first born, they will suffer less displacement with the arrival of a new baby simply because they have each other.

> _Introducing our newborn twins to my 3- and 5-year-old was the hardest part for me. I knew it would be difficult, but I didn't realize how long the adjustment would take. Everyone outside the family treated the twins as celebrities, and that always made me feel guilty. Introducing my newest baby to the twins (now 6) was easier, because they had each other for support._
> Karen Gromada, Cincinnati, OH

• Don't be surprised by regressive, jealous, or angry behavior. It's normal and better expressed rather than repressed. (Of course, it's not fun to deal with, especially since the double duty of caring for twins may be draining your energy at the same time.) Listen to—and don't chastise—negative feelings that are expressed.

• Reaffirm your older child's place in the family as the big brother/big sister. Be generous with praise and helpfulness.

• Remember that the children are all equally brothers and sisters. Don't divide them into "the twins" and "the other" children.

• Make an effort to set aside private one-on-one time for the older child, even if it means hiring two babysitters for the twins while you and your older child go out for an hour or so.

Turn To for Twin Tips

TWINS® Magazine
11211 E. Arapahoe Rd., Suite 101 Centennial, CO 80112-3851
(303) 290-8500 • Toll Free: (888)-55-TWINS (888-558-9467)
www.twinsmagazine.com. This site will lead you to other twin resources, books for parents and children, and more.

National Organization of Mothers of Twins Clubs Inc.
NOMOTC, Executive Office, P.O. Box 700860, Plymouth, MI 48170, (248) 231-4480 or (877) 540-2200, *info@nomotc.org*

• Alert visitors to your older child's need for attention. If they don't pick up on this, make a point of calling attention to the value, helpfulness, and uniqueness of the child.

• Let your older child spend the night occasionally with grandparents, relatives, or close friends, where he or she can be the center of attention. (Hopefully, your child will view this as a treat and not as a way of being shut out.)

• Some mothers of twins advise against dressing the twins identically. If you don't call attention to the fact that they're twins, they may get less special attention, and the older child will have fewer reasons to feel jealous or competitive.

Be aware that having twins is a situation that won't go away as they get older. Twins will always create interest that a singleton can't compete with. Don't forget to praise and reinforce positive behavior from a child who is trying to deal with this situation.

If Your Baby is Ill or Premature

• If you have advance warning of a problem, explain to your child that sometimes babies are not born "perfect" and will need special care or a longer hospital stay. Emphasize the fact that you are doing everything you can to improve the baby's chances by taking care of yourself with proper rest, nutrition, and exercise. Sibling classes, often sponsored by hospitals, can be helpful for explaining special circumstances to young children. Fears of the unknown are the worst, so giving your child honest information is important.

• Your child may feel cheated because the baby he or she has been promised for so long has to stay in the hospital longer than expected. Waiting is hard for small children. Do what you can to help your child practice patience.

• Explain prematurity in simple terms such as, "The baby came too soon, or he or she wasn't quite ready to be born yet." Depending on the age and maturity of your older child, you may want to be specific about the baby's problems. Be sure to include your child in the conversation with others when you share news about milestones or setbacks in the baby's progress.

• Explain the infant's illness after birth in simple enough terms that your child can understand, perhaps comparing it with an illness the child has had, if possible.

• Be aware that the child may also be worried about your health and the possibility that you will be taken away. Be as honest and reassuring about this as you can.

• Be sure your child understands that an infant's prematurity or illness is no one's fault—not yours, not the baby's and certainly not the child's. Some children feel that because they didn't want a sibling, they are to blame for the problem. Reassure your child that this isn't so.

• Be frank about the possibility of the baby's dying, if the possibility exists, explaining that it's a rare occurrence and again emphasizing that it's no one's fault.

• Encourage your child to send drawings or other offerings to the infant in the hospital.

• Include the hospitalized baby in family life at home. Talk about the baby, display pictures, play in the baby's room, have your child sit and read with you while use a breast pump, and mark a calendar with milestones of the baby's progress in the hospital.

• Let the child visit the hospital with you, and, if possible, see the baby. If the child is young, be sure someone is available to be with him or her in the waiting room. If you think the baby's appearance or the special equipment used might frighten your child, be sure to prepare him or her for it beforehand.

• If you are hospitalized longer than expected, make every effort to let your child visit so that he or she can see that you are not deathly ill. If visiting is not possible, regular telephone calls should help relieve your child's fears.

• Try to arrange for your older child to have just one caregiver while you're gone, keeping his or her routine as normal as possible. (This is also important if it will be necessary for you to visit the baby often after you've been discharged.)

• Give your older child all the special love and attention possible. He or she may resent your preoccupation with the sick baby. Tell your child you realize how little time you are able to devote to him or her because of the baby, and that feelings of resentment (even hatred) for the baby are natural and understandable.

If You Have a Miscarriage or Your Newborn Dies

Your child may be very upset after such a loss, or may not express much concern over the loss of an infant he or she has never seen. Relief at having Mom home, well and once again devoted to him or her may be the child's strongest feeling.

Be aware that questions may come later. Be receptive to them and give honest, open answers, geared to the child's age. Don't hesitate to say, "I don't know why it happened," if that's the case. Do be sure that the child knows that it was not his or her fault that the baby died, even if the child has been secretly wishing that the baby would die or go away. Remind children more than once that they are not responsible for the death.

• Do raise the issue, just to be sure there is no buried confusion, anxiety or guilt. (Did the baby die because I didn't want him or her? What happened? Will I die too?)

> *Our infant son died of crib death when our first son was 2. We were all in shock, and to our surprise, our 2-year-old cried with everyone else. We told him the baby had stopped living as we do and is now with God. Now, at 4-1/2 he still has sad moments for his baby brother. Then we think of the fun times we did share with him. And we end it with a smile.*
>
> *Kim Bricker, Park Ridge, NJ*

• If you're in the hospital with a miscarriage or a stillborn, do let your child come visit you there. Do not exclude the older sibling from the hospital vigil when a baby is struggling for survival. For a child under 5 years, fear of abandonment by the mother is very strong. In fact the greatest fear of a surviving sibling is that of being left alone. Ask if they wish to see their baby brother or sister, if that is an option.

• Be sure to let your child know it's all right to talk about the baby and to mention him or her by name. You may want to give your child a memento to remember the baby. Let your child know that grief is a normal emotion that does not pass quickly. Don't hesitate to seek professional help for yourself or your child if you think it's necessary.

• Explain where the stillborn's body is, or your child will fantasize incorrectly to its whereabouts. It's okay to visit the grave site, too.

• Be tolerant of behavior changes in your child such as clinging, whining, aggressiveness, bed-wetting and nightmares. Recognize that they are temporary responses to stress. Give your child all the love and attention you can.

• Help your child realize that unintentional hurtful comments he or she overhears—_"It's for the best," "You can have other children," "At least you didn't get to know the baby"_—are not meant to be unkind but are made by people who don't understand and don't know what to say.

• If the child is old enough, let him or her mourn with you and attend the funeral (if appropriate). Don't isolate yourself in your grief, however hard it is. Share your sorrow with your family.

You're Not Alone so Don't Be Alone

Support groups and resource are an absolute must at times like this. Call, and encourage anyone you know dealing with such a sadness, to use any available. The Internet is a wonderful resource for finding the support you need. Here are just a few, for starters:

SHARE: Pregnancy and Infant Loss Support
St. Joseph Health Center
300 First Capital Dr., St. Charles, MO 63301
(800-821-6819) *http://nationalshareoffice.com*

NO NEW BABY by Marilyn Gryte. In this book, a loving and caring grandmother explains to her grandchild. "You're not to blame," it's okay to ask questions and that adults do not always have the answers. Available from SHARE.

First Candle/SIDS Alliance Inc. *(Sudden Infant Death Syndrome)*
1314 Bedford Ave # 210, Baltimore, MD 21208
(800-221-7437) *www.sidsalliance.org*
Other SIDS sites: www.sids-network.org and www.sids.org

EMPTY CRADLES
Internet support for miscarriage, stillbirth, infant loss, and SIDS.
www.empty-cradles.com

CHAPTER SEVEN

And What About Me?

❧

As you have discovered, a second pregnancy does differ from the first. You can be very tired, have morning sickness and have everyone excited for you. But the excitement is less than for your first child. Others may be critical of your timing and wonder (or even asked) if this was your plan. Even your husband or partner may not show as much excitement as you saw with your first child. You will probably not be given a baby shower and you will have less time to focus on this pregnancy.

Your body will probably react differently in this pregnancy in some ways. You will probably look pregnant sooner, have more frequent Braxton-Hicks contractions and your delivery may go faster.

But you are more secure knowing what lies ahead. This next baby may or may not be easier than your first but by now you basically know what to do and what to expect. And you will have the fun of sharing the arrival of this new baby with your older child(ren).

It may be harder to make time for yourself but you've made the major adjustment to the fact that parenthood has already changed your private time. The most common way moms make time for themselves (after the baby is on a regular schedule) is to wake a half hour before the rest of the family to carve out that niche of personal time.

Preparing Yourself for Some Changes in Lifestyle

• Time spent in a childbirth refresher course can be a good investment in preparing for the changes ahead. It's also good quality time to spend with your partner.

• Life getting too stressful? Recognize that although pregnancy may be a natural condition, it puts an enormous strain on you physically. Cut back and make time to give your body the rest it needs; adjust your diet to include the nutrients you and your baby both need.

• Be aware that mothers can pick up a toddler until the last part of their pregnancy unless the doctor advises otherwise. Lifting may affect your back, but not your unborn baby.

• If you can't pick the child up, provide a little stool for getting into and out of the high chair, crib or bed. Hug your toddler often when you're sitting down or playing on the floor.

• Expect a tantrum or crying jag when you leave your child if you haven't left the child very often. Children do experience separation anxiety but don't let this stop you. Most tantrums end within 10 minutes after you leave.

Before Delivery Details

• Get your house baby-ready BEFORE you deliver. Stock up on diapers, wipes, baby shampoo and the like. Assemble baby gear.

• Give both hand-me-down clothes and new baby clothes a run through your washing machine.

• Buy or make a supply of frozen meals.

• Set up an account with an online, grocery delivery service. It will be helpful.

• Have a good supply of healthy snacks (like granola bars) and individual bottles of water and juice boxes on hand for both you and your older child.

• Using paper cups and plates is perfectly okay for a few weeks until life settles in. Let go of your expectations of yourself for a while. Everything DOESN'T have to get done immediately.

• Write out a message for your phone voice mail system to use once you get home. Then don't feel you have to answer every ring.

The Postpartum Doula

For second time parents the days and weeks after birth can be a juggling act worthy of a Barnum and Bailey circus. Recognizing the traits of a rapidly changing newborn is less stressful once you've seen it all before, but the simultaneous demands of housework, an older child, meals, and errands can put any parent over the top. An excellent solution is the postpartum doula. Postpartum simply means "following birth" and "doula" is the Greek word for the 'woman of the home's own female servant.' Today's postpartum doulas are experienced with the changes and adjustments of a family with a newborn. The doula helps juggle the daily household tasks so a mother—and father—can have more time to be with their baby and each other. And there is more time to rest—a necessity for recovery. The postpartum doula understands newborn characteristics, family needs, and when to call the doctor. The doula's non-judgmental and flexible support helps parents be more successful in adapting, can make breast feeding successful, and give mom greater self-confidence and have fewer postpartum issues. One can hire a doula for a few hours a day or the whole day.

Information on postpartum doulas is available from DONA International. Call toll free at 1-888-788-3662 or check online at www.dona.org.

Telling Your Boss You're Pregnant

When to tell your boss you are pregnant is a politically sensitive situation. If you wait too long, you can cause your superior to loose trust in you and cause yourself or your boss embarrassment especially if you were being counted on for a specific project. If your announcement is very early, you might find yourself being passed over for certain assignments if your company doesn't feel you can be counted on. Being honest about what your plans are and your interest in continuing your work commitment needs to be shared. The law doesn't require a woman to disclose her pregnancy but if you wish to make a strong case for working while pregnant and returning after maternity leave, disclose the facts as soon as you are sure of them. If, on the other hand you have a lower wage job, you may wish to wait longer before you share your news as lower wage jobs often expect turn over and jobs are not always held for you.

Preparing to Go Back to Work

• Combine your vacation time and maternity leave time to give yourself as much time home with your family as possible.

• Keep in touch with coworkers while you are home so you have a sense of what is going on at work.

• Set up a meeting with your boss once you hone in on your return date. Maybe there is even a project you can do by email to ease you back into the work place.

• Cook and freeze meals ahead to make those first few weeks easier.

• If nursing, pump and freeze more breast milk than you think you'll need before returning to work.

• Go in to the office part-time, without pay, for a few days to give you a chance to ease in on your terms.

• Start your return midweek so that your first week is really only half a week.

• Pick your baby doctor convenient to either your home or daycare to make visits easier to work into your schedule.

• If your older child has been in daycare while you've been working, it's okay to have that child continue when you are home with your baby, if finances allow. It is good for everyone.

• Start your new daycare/sitter arrangements a few days or so before starting back to work to make sure it is going smoothly. It will also give you time to get a few things done before you start your new schedule.

Emotional Adjustments

For some moms, that first day, or first week are the toughest. Others find the first days easy but it becomes harder after a few weeks. Don't be too hard on yourself as you make your own back-to-work adjustment.

• Join a support group for parents in your workplace, if available. Or just seek out other moms to talk to over lunch to compare notes and feelings.

• Call your daycare provider or sitter as often as you need to in the early weeks.

• Feeling slightly jealous of your child's caretaker is normal. Remember that babies always know who mommy and daddy are.

And What About a Third Child?

While most couples today do stop at number two, there is a modest increase reported in third pregnancies. Some are calling "three, the new two." Several factors are behind this: advances in fertility treatments mean women can consider a 3rd child in their 40s or they may have a multiple birth; caring for three kids is becoming more manageable as employers allow more 'flex' time and have more family-friendly policies. And many couples like to try for that other gender child if their first two are the same sex.

But having a third child has a strong economic impact that needs to be considered. Yes, you have another daycare and college education to pay for. There are other 'hidden' expenses to consider too. Will you need a larger home with another bedroom? Will you now need a minivan? The world we live in is made for four, not five when it comes to getting a cab, a table at a restaurant or needing an extra room when on vacation. Even a family suite may only accommodate four.

The joys of three or more can be multiple, however!

Index